After projects the resound

Kimberly Alidio

for Margaret, likewise and in mutuality; love, Kimberly

ISBN: 978-0-9964001-8-3

1. American poetry—21st century. 2. Poets, American—21st Century.

Black Radish Books
www.blackradishbooks.com

First printing 2016 in the United States of America

Cover art: Gina Osterloh, *Blank Athleticism, Turquoise Room #1* 48″×60″ Lightjet 2007.

Book design and layout: Black Radish Books

Distributed by:
Small Press Distribution
1341 Seventh Street
Berkeley, CA 94710-1409
spd@spdbooks.org

Contents

After projects the resound

The ash does not add

Let's say this smell in my palm is your scalp's.
An archive
And someone is lying about how we have been to each other
How a life is a living
            built

Suddenly you're old, waiting and trying
I've been looking past the crown of your baby hairs for a good while now
Here is time.

I think of a boat: deliverance
            betraying every word for a building

            Walking through
            these landscapes muted and
            mishearing
            perpetually pre-words
            I go by smell

            You would think I would
            gather some bright
            haloes
            behind baby hairs
            deserving much
            mercy

I'm too dumb for the category

            All bodies are pressed grease
            drying down to
            bone   I become
            your crackle pop

The disorder of preserving is
absolutely not the fracture
Just run-of-the-mill jus soli treason
unsponsored
beyond relative
bounds

reading
re-reading
re-reading and

I am brought close to bear the difference
safe from calls to discord
held tight

I want to be common.

"The whole thing is this"
I want you to shut up until you have something in your arms

I'll close my eyes

Now I will behold a whole tropical story

That is how father the seeds are light colored not deep brown when you open the fruit
We serve and ripen the stimulating oils
In high excitement as though they instead of their master were going to the fiesta
Then shepherd ate the berries too and felt stimulated himself.
Why we are twice as likely to excite ourselves to a quick ecstasy
Are we the stars of the party not collateral damage
In a dream my tender torso pinned snugly with fast shards
Flown Chinese stars show in a picture
February emerges with Hello Kitty's rubber title and panels of Spam
Teething a chip of the father chatter on surf in Hawaii
Exits six chambers truckle to caesura
A cloudy hard palate through the left cerebral and occipital
I know replies Daddy of all the states
The nicest smell is California's

Doll

the heart structure has a home-and-family-feeling
anyone's dustier clone
can prompt feelings for damaged nerves
anatomies highways and all more or less above the subatomic
doll themselves up into systems
a whole flooding province toys with a satellite labor camp
mini knock-offs
mass migrations mass produce at a scale beyond the eye
any one person gets lost along the way
but a story projects domesticated edges
back bent I stroke the yellow shag down
to make way for a paper doll water buffalo and poor cousin
I like to pretend I'm a giant
my numbness is a publican mood
I hover over my girlfriends grooming them with identical bowl cuts
settling needs small-scale operations not ornaments
when I see a real-life chair I think
what makes this work is the accident of my size

The lack the whole

the checklist of our discipline's grammar

the viscous products of grandmotherly brooms

the acids of our ethnic backwash

are you my dear one walking on earth

my lowercase

my salutary beloved
            mercantile trader
                        ship from afar

(I hope you brought blankets)

Servants

Continued rescuing a train wreck refusing for a head

Wound Sole survivor of a smallpox epidemic on a drifting into an

Island

Some proof that congressmen drank aboard to Panama. Bound and

Gagged as the gang a string of 213 perfect pearls. His employer committed him, a

Decision deemed forty years later a likely

Of a jewel after midnight the women of Freeport wanted to their

Husbands Sponsored by a discharged chaplain, at the

St. Alphonsus Church Fair.

Instead of leaving the quarters knocked

To the ground. A leper forced onto the with 124 horses and mules

Requisitioned for the quartermaster. Denied

his employer's clothing. Seeing

A bruised on the stairs In her bare feet. Saw acts. Employer

May have her into a room and the door. Said a freedwoman and

Fellow also shipped by the to the islands and back but in

Doubt about her own birth and the Meaning of perjury. Passed

Out in a room from gas

but enough to Sail the

Next day. Committee on and janitors ordered to Decide:

Or white? Buoyed by a news article

his employer searching for him

Fled revolutionaries and Seeking at the legation. Boasted of

To a local woman, sparking Heated at the barracks.

Left Fort Bliss,

Beaten. Entered his Employer's caught her hands as she

Clad in a shapeless and raw grass jacket. Followed her through

Honolulu unimpressed.

As we go missing

maps entail and despair
proximity orientation direction scale
a perfect shell stretched windowpanes
from cellular to worm warm
from bloody river shed to tongue cleaned
        dismembered
        like weedy tops
robot dead inside
the penetrating maps
inner life collapsed out
just like an interlude
        counterpoint
        organ grinder
menstrual map rosy from an ensemble response
set off a composition
picked clean like weeds
scale the tongue
        the pattern
                the pattern
        the pattern

AKA

bija, bijol (Taino), bixa orrellana, bixaceae (Latin botaniko), biksa, biksa orel'ina (Ruso), bjoul, orleanfa, ruku (wika ng Unggarya), orlean-drvo (wika ng Serbya), orleanbaum, orleansamen, orleanstrauch (Aleman), chacuanguarica, pumacua (Puerto Rico), urucu (Tupi), urucu bravo, urucu da mata, urucum, açafroa, açafrao, açafroeira, da terra, colorau (Portuges sa Brazil), roucou (wika ng Karibe, wika ng Olandes), foucou (wika ng Karibe), woukou rocou (Kreola), roucouyer (Pranses), daagyene, konin (Akan-Asante), dagyiri (Brong), djanfarana (Crioulo), djambarana (Fula-Pulaar), anatta (Puerto Rico), annatto (Ingles, Aleman, Italyano), a-na-to (Koreano), anoto (Portuges sa Brazil), onoto (Venezuela), anatoo, be ni no ki (Hapon), annatobusken (wika ng Dinamarka), annatopoosa (wika ng Estonia), annattosamen, anattostrauch (Aleman), arnatto (wika ng Turkiya), aarnatu (Kannada), arnota, arnota właściwa (wika ng Polonya), lipsticktree (Ingles), hong mu, yan zhi shu (wika ng Tsina), latkan, lotkan, sindure (wika ng Bengal), sendri, shendri (wika ng Maharashtra), sinduri (wika ng Gujarat), gowpurgee, senduria, sinduria (Hindi), sindurpushpi, shonapushpi, trivapushpi, virpushpa (Sanskrit), sindur (wika ng Nipál), dieu nhuom, ht iu mau, siem phung (wika ng Biyetnam), burek, burk (wika ng Palaw), loa loa (wika ng Samoa), 'alaea, 'alaea la'au, kūmauna (wika ng Hawai'i), 'uaeva (wika ng Maori), 'uaefa (wika ng Tahiti), jarak belanda, kesum, kesumba, kesumba kling, kunyit jawa, sumpeh, suntak (wika ng Malaya), galuga (Arabe, Indonesyo), galinggem (Sundanese), achiotl (Nahuatl), achiote (Nahuatl, Maya, Chamorro, wika ng Bulgarya, Olandes, Espanyol, Pranses), achioytello (Espanyol), achihuite (wika ng Colombia), achoti (Chamorro), a chi o te, a-c-io-te, bik sa sok (Koreano), achiti, asuite, atsuite (Iloko), achote (Tagalog, Espanyol, Panama), achoete (Tagbanwa), atswete (Tagalog, Sambali, Bikolano, Ilokano, Panay Bisaya), atsiute (Sambali), chanang, janang (Sulod), chotes (Samar-Leyte Bisaya), sotis (Cebu Bisaya), asuti (Tagalog), asoti (Ibanag), apactut (Ga'dang)

To turn insurgents into state agents

Till and fertilize and plant brand new grass

Make breathing space

Drain the swamps from which the pests arise

Whack the weeds getting too high

"You have the watches but we have the time"

Keep soil from eroding after pulling the weeds

It's not plinking away from above or just mowing the grass

Daddy Burger Snow Copernicus

a riverfront breezes the downed twin towers

edison plays with tub toys in jersey

black bars over his eyes some reminder

glory the inglorious riot the twentieth c.

a drafty set piece sequenced in drapery and gels

don't forget the maine in a revel a lust

our silence a sour exhale tracking dust and gas

dictatorships replace my fascia every seven years

more warp speed than revenge of the half-lady

my ghost walking queer and brown for pay

I'll take a husband for the occident alex

what is trading tenses for hemispheres

what is rice paddy repatriation

what fruits my fatty skin

Only mangos and jungle

Be with girls now pick a lady
Speak only mangos and jungle

Tremble the untouchable
The way is approximate

A pickle touch blackens
This avenue of kings

Charlotte and Florence
Soft-elbow a hunt

A chance trip forking
Blanketed snow

Unfit alter states force
Copper ears and cannon eye

Left hand off the wrist
Leapt onto the ground an ex

An open stream down
Throats sparkles dilation

Torture a tender missive
Maker my making

In the province

their president mildewing

where copra pays nothing now

nor hemp cigars rice or sugar

pick them out their Sunday best

enter their homes

eat their grade A beef

ripen there or else rot

be bright and reverb fan flag five four

calm your horse slip among stats

arise fully dressed filling like hammocks

monkeyshine soft pouched sucking

falling into trance insisting

repeat hum muddle-sop

Fermented AKA ferment

Catch-up katsup catsip cotsup kotchup kitsip catsoup katshoup
Katsock cackchop cotpock kutpuck kutchpuck Heinz ketchup
Del Monte catsup Hunt's catsup east of the Mississippi Hunt's
Katchup west of the Mississippi Hunt's cornchops Iowa only
Ge-tchup ke-tsiap koe-cheup kue-chiap in old Hokkien 300 BC
After bartering on sampans sailed from Guangdong's kingdom
Of Nan Han and Fujian's kingdom of Min into Nanying
Ports of Champa Cambodia Ilocos Visaya Sumatra and Java
Made kecap nuoc mam nam pla patis made colonial empire
Get its taste from the fermented fish zone to sail back to pirate
Umami 1699 OEDs catchup a high East India sauce as expensive
As tea try a ferment of celery plum Jane Austen's unripe walnut
Kidney bean 1711 Lockyer's travel account OEDs ketchup a fine
Export from Tonqueen Tonquin Tonkin Tongkin Tongking try a
Ferment of love-apple peach lemon elderberry mushroom anchovy
Mussel one hundred oysters a gallon of stale beer 1804 Culina
Famulatrix Medicinæ advises tomatas too rare pulp turmeric
And apple in good imitation 1876 Heinz in America passes
21 CFR 155.194 OEDs ketchup catsup catchup high fructose
Corn syrup gallon of vinegar red and reddish Lycopersicum
Non-Newtonian liquid Reagan-vegetable for the small fry

I'm opening a square of burr oaks

archon is neon a juniper's spoil
and resolve some quiet carpet
boring exterior weird interiors
robes hold the body in blinking shimmer
translucent race a sensible haircut
our accrual in a place ruled by forms
gestures are techniques to root around senses
an archaic quality a little stringy
elongate as much as possible a fiscal return
our practitioner body disappears from the sight line
signal goodbye clog-walking the outer season
mollusk mucus is my sort of remark
across typeface sharply unprepared
a dumb yelp trailing you

Our lady of the banana ketchup

a guava jelly a food scientist
a Maria Y. Orosa a world war # 2
a gut sucking a powdered soybean
a concentration camp a claypot oven
a lime-ash soap a rice-bran cookie
a cassava flour a green banana flour
a heart hit twice by shrapnel
a sodium benzoate
a heroine of the soyalac
a sauce for the succulent belly
a saba a banana a yellow # 6
a red # 40 a sugar a vinegar
a UFC a Jufran a Mother's Best
a torta a hipster a hotdog spaghetti
a hater a sweeter tomato

Memoir

Acting a saint with saucer-eyes under Sally Struthers' armpit
A flat-roofed house and a south-facing wall of sliding doors
After a drought, mosquitos late in October
Ankles and shoulders stinging simultaneously in rich neighborhoods
Around the time of the war, a schoolhouse without chairs
Asking freely do you promise
At the dinner table, a monologue and insomnia
At the river, another white guy bringing up napalm

Big labor men, wise guys
The backseat a full-length fur coat
Blood sugar getting low
Binding our husking thighs together like Rosemary's Baby
The boy who'd stole my car sending me money from prison
Breaking the routine of going to meetings of awful people
The bridge slats with spaces just wide enough to catch small feet on the way to the outhouse
Brushing off bugs, which rubs them into the skin
By the time I'm wiping myself, you chatting in the highest register

Chair squeak, a leaning sound
The chained monkey
Changing the subject only slightly to dream of Patty Hearst bringing down Goldman Sachs
City blocks during a long ride in a 1984 Lincoln Town Car
Climbing trees for breakfast after oversleeping
Cortisone at home
Cory Aquino taking my hand and asking for a donation of my weekly allowance

The deep craters lice carve into old books becoming terraced over time

Flatly reading out the words under the loud plastic dust jacket for an oral book report
The film stopping for three minutes
Finding what she said really resonates

Getting who we are but not this place where we're surrounded by hinterland
Giving everything you own to a pink corner house in North Beach with a baroque chapel on
the second floor
Giving up trying to take fan-girl photos of black writers on stage

Having kids because you've been kidnapped
His returning her
Her arriving during winter crying
Her name Bernardina before she got sick
Her handling the unfired clay
Her forgetting to get off the bus
Her moving by increments into the wheelchair
Her never growing tall
Her new name after recovering
Her slurring from chemo and weed
Her speaking for a grandfather who in his day loved his Moros
His family still running scared long after returning to the city

Inventing a place-machine to drop spawn over the fence

The John Sayles film "Amigo" premiering in Manila at the same time
Just one kid bringing a red lacquered chair

Knotting an undershirt into a turban to weather yesterday's thunderstorm on the way here

Learning to abide the pull of little men
The local paper naming him as her survivor

More than a few declaring a desire to move out of the country
Mosquitos that know you
Most people in the transcripts preferring a better alias
My distant family giving me the room with the gold satin sheets

My great-aunties lovers since their teens
My writing a letter of apology

No one thinking to take pictures of the house they grew up in
Not making any counterclaims
Nude on the couch and pretending he's never waved hello through the window

Of all the bars in the world right now, the sound of a poet's shiny pate
Otherwise remaining undiscovered
Over a century of Twain complaining loudly of the lack of good information about the
    Philippines
Our course-correcting by delivering our babies to the world's lesbians and gay men who keep
their rent-controlled apartments after they die
Our mistake bearing kids where we were born
Our talking about Chinese Caribbean food like old friends
Our working to the bone to make lazy children in one generation

People beyond the fence yelling
A piece of air-mail wedged in the pantry between How to Cook with Imported San Miguel
    Beer and Easy Recipes for the First Homemaker with the New Teflon Pan
Pilgrimaging to see the razed site of the I-Hotel, for a while a hole in the middle of a
    financial district
Pink ribbons busy shrinking that meanie
A poet I know from the internet shifting in his chair
A priest on retainer

Rainclouds and his tortilla soup making a vivid republic
Rows of soundless turbines

Sally Mann for seven years naked and surrounded by packs of dogs
Sensing a thighbone rotating closer
Stumbling a second too long over the word TSAR
So that interesting talk

Some people knowing me on the internet
Someone presenting a video exposé on air-borne diseases of people squatting on trash
    mountains

Telling her to call me up to have tea
That great movie, say
Then missing her
Their banking on their one visit as burial
Their living in one house until they didn't
Their using labor recruitment, marriage sponsorship, and church activity to live together,
    grow spinach, and watch Lawrence Welk
This apology belonging to no one
Travis County Juvenile Corrections calling for my address

A veil pinning them and she squares her jaw
The Virgin visiting no matter what you're called now

Wanting to fall asleep
What's left from rotten holes is an archipelago
When I touch the sheets, hearing a rooster's crow
Where Bulosan used to drink
Where the gambling dens were
With copper pennies, making bicultural concessions to replenish after loss
With strangers intoning "Rappin' with Ten Thousand Carabaos in the Dark"
Without it our running before we drop
A woman nearby texting
Wondering whether the new generation of iPhone cameras is any better at capturing dark
    skinned faces, especially under harsh auditorium lights

You're given to gold filigree and poverty vows
Your identifying as a feminist taking anti-birth control mission trips to Mexico
Your smelling yourself under the girl mess
Your startling someone holding a conversation with herself

A history of migraines links to transient global amnesia

paper must keep
best loved at 70 degrees F and 50% RH
sweat must evaporate
static film discolors her facial recto
mini-spatula and nitrile mitt might
gentle her soft the rag
rag paper holy of hostesses
damp turns her into a nest
do you remember your migraine
fluorescence jitters
do you know the person who came with you to the hospital
skin thickens detains glass & cactus
I believe in one market
limp banknotes giving a history of our touch

Enclosed within a boundary

Muster rolls NAVAC Serial File of 1950 ltrs N1-1(1)
Reconstruction of Guam Courtmartials Scandalous
Conduct Tending to Destruction of Morals CHARGE I:
(LASCIVIOUS) (seven specifications) Finding: proved
SENTENCE: Confined for a period of five years CHARGE II:
SODOMY proved by plea Guilty SENTENCE: Confined
for a period of ten years To be dishonorably discharged
Place, expanse, the extent of a two-dimensional surface
CHARGE III: CONDUCT TO THE PREJUDICE OF GOOD
ORDER AND DISCIPLINE (two specifications) One spec
with a beast, carabao Finding: not proved. Here
is the transcription of the first page marked RESTRICTED
Do not want to bother getting a sticker to copy it
On or over and with a leg on each side of a blank area
Continue looking in box 12 of 12. The unmarked folder
with reproduction tab 2 S-P-E-E-D-L-E-T-T-E-R
"Write your name in the space provided"
Tropical records have rusty paper clips
White MacBook coated with fine brown dust
Present intentions are that these people will return
to Honolulu upon completion of current contracts
Pertaining to or emanating from a labyrinth
Heave phlegm into the bathroom trash
From ComMarianas To: Distribution List

Primly inside a melon zone

Liking is starting a fight with another feeling
Creased between inner and Lakeshore
              He dreams in terms of skyscrapers.
                            Girls
                            like them.
                            Mature women liked them. Everybody.

Not shocked enough about purveyor girls
With full access to our living quarters.

                      Do your memories begin
                            with
                      Perhaps my first
                            clear memory
                 is standing
                            on the deck of a transport peering through the railing
                            wishing
                            the horn would blow

Cento

If it pushes too hard   the story is over too fast
a closed death   At the end of it all you end up

It felt to me   not being dead for one

I never minded being   I fall I flow I melt
Story & measure—from the primal pool   of the shared grave

Love involves not being dead for the other
Misery or joy engulfs me   passing as

I am dissolved, not dismembered   and so of course I
re-entered   re-

without any particular tumult ensuing   nor any pathos
This is exactly what gentleness is

dragging everything up whole—

Certainty is a kind of desire

I'm certain I sense the space around the objects in the room because I'm often unnoticed

Unnoticed objects and the unnoticed space around them sense one another in a moment of shared indifference to the room's manners that a room enforces to understand a room

A table setting where space gets caught in things

I'm not certain that space around objects attracts my attention because attention is its own desire and there's space around it that does not attract attention

I don't want to be more certain about negative space than the object in negative space

I don't want mastery over every object and everyone's attention

I want to jump from an endowed hall to a dinner table to a sea cliff

How does one enter a room if there is nothing sovereign in the space around you that attracts attention

I tried to write about them to be proper company for myself

Precarious, temporary, transient

Who never meant to stay in a place long enough to build anything, left negligible and unexceptional traces

For whom everything is laid out in foundations on top of newly fresh massacres

Everything promised: democracy-discipline, preservation-radical future, reform-commemoration, technology-money, radical study-surface pleasure

Who is served yet unquenched, still quenched, absorbed

Represented, found, counted in their time and ours

Who before leaving were prompted to leave ephemera for others to collect into cavernous libraries with a special elevator for the half floors for others to have the goods, the new names

To stop being lonely in a lonely obscure language while staying mute in the people's language.

January 5	Plaza Dancing Hall	85	Phillipinos
January 24	Plaza Dancing Hall	95	Phillipinos
February 16	Plaza Dancing Hall	70	Phillipinos
February 17	Mayfair Dancing Hall	50	Phillipinos and Japanese
June 22	Plaza Dancing Hall	90	Phillipinos
June 16	Mayfair Dancing Hall	80	Phillipinos
June 25	Mayfair Dancing Hall	100	Orientals and Phillipinos
July 14	Mayfair Dancing Hall	65	Phillipinos and Japanese
August 4	Plaza Dancing Hall	75	Phillipinos
August 8	Mayfair Dancing Hall	85	Phillipinos
August 18	Plaza Dancing Hall	67	Phillipinos
October 10	New American Dancing Hall #2	100	Phillipinos
October 11	New American Dancing Hall #2	50	Phillipinos
October 11	Madison-Ashland Dancing Hall	3	Phillipinos
October 12	New American Dancing Hall #2	10	Phillipino
October 12	Empire Dancing Hall	20	Phillipinos
October 12	Colonial Dancing Hall	5	Phillipinos
October 13	New American Dancing Hall #2	150	Phillipinos
October 13	Mayfair Dancing Hall	75	Phillipinos
October 13	Plaza Dancing Hall	85	Phillipinos

Showing up in groups every night or every week to pay to dance with women and to gamble, they drew the attention of

Crime reporters, naturalists, radicals, examiners, prosecutors, poverty tourists, predatory lenders, smugglers, friends of the friendless, rescuers of white slaves, bohemian writers, embarrassed independence leaders, cops

the outer peel
the hanging skin
the maws
the slacken

the story
all at once
a mark, a tactic, a partisan tract

A serious researcher never sees the ordinary

In ordinary life, permanent personality types are property of private aggravations

Oceans of armed submarines are lined with quaint transports:

How spectacular a desire is his crossing!

To be at arms length. To feel his breathing.

An out-of-towner though seeds the public.

When it first opened, one early problem was what attitude to take towards the prostitutes in the community. It was obvious they were friends of ________ and used to meeting them elsewhere. They ate here at first and angered us with their coarse conversations and laughter. Their presence secured to make ________ just like any other joint. Then they began to come into the living room. There were rumors that they even got upstairs in the sleeping quarters. At any rate, the idea of their having free access to the house at any time was very revolting to me and I decided we might do something about it. Mr. ________'s attitude toward these women was first one of unconcern or at least so it seemed. At any rate, he did not show any anxiety and feeling of revulsion.

Dwell in the mood of mechanical gestures

Space out

Forget the current condition

Be alone in public

Adopt new devotional obsessions

Self-medicate

Interrupt the belabored life-building

Repeat the outcomes

Use up family savings, language skills, social manners, national pride, letters of recommendation

Bet against the house, women working the late shift, on diminished credit

Lose the political debts

Janitorial, back-of-the-house, broken-English, bottom-rung work of the highly groomed houseboy

Any grounds for legitimate, temporary residence in the city

To lose this face

Each pathology has an institution worthy of it

Over four hundred suitcases are found in the New York psychiatric hospital attic when it closes down. In the way of civic and popular memory, exhibits of patient suitcases seek to recover something from disaster. Most patients were immigrants without family ties who came into conflict with someone—a landlord or a restaurant owner—during the Great Depression. About half spent their entire lives in the institution and were buried in unmarked graves.

Hospital staff members labeled patients' belongings and stored them in alphabetical order, organized by sex. Patient #15902 has a suitcase containing a handwritten autobiography about his American schooling; a handwritten novella; an Illinois Naval Reserve wardroom boy's cap; a color postcard from Mackinac Island, Michigan; textbooks like A Primer of Industry; and a photograph of a student gathering under a festooned portrait of a famous nationalist.

Every racialized, colonial, migrant, working-class pathology has its own confinement, theft and sensational plot

Born in Capiz at the turn of the twentieth-century. Came to the U.S. under care of a Protestant organization for relocated children in Salt Lake City, Utah. Moved to Buffalo as a house servant for a prominent doctor. Started to hear voices calling him a sinner after a romance with a young woman fell apart. Employer committed him. Diagnosed with syphilis.

Sociable, readily converses with anyone, plays checkers, displays interest in life, takes it upon himself to guide a disabled Japanese American patient to each meal, volunteers with yard work, regularly patronizes the hospital library, writes simple poetry. Polite, mannerly, cooperative, neat and clean, never causes trouble, a señor. Seeks the protection of the hospital walls when he hears voices while outdoors. Foregoes drug or electro-shock treatments. Keeps up letters to fellow students in the U.S.

The fifty-one years of institutionalization appear to have been a mistake, as far as duration, as this man appears in perfect mental condition now.

Old things provoke because they're not done with us yet

We came to this country to conduct ourselves as freemen.

We came here to work hard to earn an honorable living.

We came here because we would like to see what the western civilization is.

We are exceedingly glad because you brought us here in order that we might learn more than we have already learned at home.

But we are sorry to say that our desires have not been fully granted.

We wish you to treat us fairly and squarely.

We wish to have both political and civil rights.

We wish to be free and not slaves, and we wish to be under a government of the people, by the people and for the people.

A U.S. federal program to finance a one-way trip home was public sympathy

Fifteen percent of all the transported came from prisons, mental asylums, hospitals

The disorder on the part of those the historical record only suspiciously considers human

Is 2008 like 1929. Is family immigrant detention like internment. Is deportation like deportation. Is calling a place a territorial possession like building a soft hospice.

The heft and random array of objects and their geographic dispersal

Twelve articles with an approximate weight of 1010 pounds at a home in Pennsylvania.

The law says the transported have no rooting things. Just a suitcase, several boxes, perhaps a typewriter. Go home and write us a letter all about what you left behind.

$5.40 to the Bureau of Public Welfare to defray the cost of recovery.

That in addition to the 2 trunks and 3 boxes, there are among Mr. ________'s effects several hundred pounds of junk—old iron, rusty scrap, clock springs, et. Moreover, there is one large packing box containing nothing but miscellaneous books and this box and contents weigh several hundred pounds. And that as a matter of fact it would seem that the junk should be condemned and destroyed.

Things become artifacts or relics by being possessed

Abstract concepts are both objects and objectives

Venereal disease and failed romance, working as a wardroom boy for the U.S. navy and loving the country encircled by the navy's magic

Visitors behold objects with wonder, even love

The people have a bad habit of announcing their presence, place, and property after a war

Before they appear to disappear from the city

After the war they take cheap jobs in the building trades and claim to rebuild islands across the empire

They always remade into the familiar new, the next generation, the future

A mini city, a microcosm of a neocolony

2 dance halls
6 social clubs
3 tennis clubs
4 musical clubs
4 dry cleaners
2 restaurants
6 barbershops
2 pool halls
3 newspapers
2 apartment houses
1 grocery store
3 tailor shops
2 radio stores
1 photograph studio

On a map on my kitchen wall I mark places that existed in 1925
Dots ringed downtown
Now the northwest corner of the United Center
Now a vacant lot
Now the Kennedy Expressway
Now the Kruger Gallery next to the Frontera Grill
(In 1947 the Metallic Letter Company)
Now a biomedical lab at Pritzker Medical School
Now a People's Auto Parking garage

I'd found a book published in 1925 on a city
I took a train to that city
I took the book out when I got there
With the map in the inside flap I made my way from the train station to a university
I found more books on the city
I made copies
After four hours I left

Dots for each name and address clustered around local stops on north-south streets of hotels, restaurants and private homes

One couple did domestic work as a team, their names a number funneled into a larger statistic

Two went to a YMCA Christmas dinner, one enrolled in the Hamilton College of Law, the other in UIUC

Two couples lived together

Four couples and three children lived above where Madigan's used to be

A widower and two children lived there before someone filed for their repatriation

I cross-referenced a box on someone's kitchen table with a city historical file

"You'll find the Lithuanian social-realist artist here but none of your kind"

The woman who kept the box on her kitchen table called my days full of leisure

The landlord raised the rent

People live attached to acreage

We warn ourselves to concern and reform

Impossible to get evidence concerning nature of dancing as white person is conspicuous.
The anonymous person is essentially a non-moral person.

Seven days a week sometimes you take your book try to read on the elevated
You read or you fall down sleepy.

Very seldom is one of them asked to a good home.

I memorized the names and addresses
Of all the bars I went to
From the elevated to attic to archive
It's better to write directly to a place
So our writing ventriloquizes the place
From which we write
The place of our body
When the libraries closed
I went to new friends' houses
To gossip about the city
I looked at the train maps
Pinned to their kitchen walls
My finger traced the same 1925 train line
To my body's present location

The state is assumed as a shape to be filled

Which captures which?

The administration records itself impress a sense of administration if occulted

I'm supposed to unravel this

There's no origin of something already debunked in the present moment about that past in that foreign place.

I suppressed this sense for some kind of verbiage. It's now all over in name and deed

I can't find the original moment of inventing a politics as a web of relations between nation and nation, race and race, subject and subject

The web relating reason and unreason

The map that meets the untrodden space

The word engaged in the sense

Just give me a pen and long hours and an IV line stuck into my arm. I'll write it down.

We've known for a while that some were commissioned to represent and order us to form policy so some of us could become self-possessed and some of us marked for extinguishing.

They were commissioned to become immersed among the ungoverned and even get a little lost in the surround.

The documentation left behind as they traveled among us is a thinking-feeling map that people have decided is important enough to preserve in big libraries

The investigating self is resigned to be the occasion for sporting interrogation

Why are you here? What do you want?

Never new, never virginal. Seen before. A repeated pattern.

Just as it has been said in children's stories about the war of conquest when boy adventurers wander into the jungle beyond the bounds of the military fort

The immigrant colony overwhelms.

Invisible hunchbacked little person with a disfigured face

The melting pot expects

Becoming crippling indeed

What can a body do to form relations

What doesn't permit

Calls for a new intimate drilling

Even risk

This isn't ethics

It's walking together

In this writing and reading

Sensate connections already possible

A little willing to be possessed by things

The historical records do not lend themselves to illumination and enlightenment

They offer feeling against disorder

I've disappeared from making pronouncements about policy into society where I am among those who receive

You haven't noticed since I'm sort of replaceable and simultaneously unnoticeable and conspicuous among those with their secret way of speaking freely

Let's disinvest from any cause

Let's reconcile to making useless texts that refuse a certain sense of orderly argument

The way the philosopher indicates a closing of eyes

He imagines

Inhaling in an essence

Delicious apples

The distant sadness

“captive”

The way I earn that line

Sometimes a shrug will do it

Brushing a close by

Other times a shudder you’re marked

I shiver your company

I morsel you

Do you want vitamins?

Dental floss!
Shampoo! Soup! Cereal! Instant coffee!
Bubblegum to turn your mouth blue!
An African thumb drum!
Corn! Dirt bike! Fish bait!
Blue shoes, possibly unisex!
Pink bath set.
What things look like in Canada.
My employer's baby clothes.
My shiny doll face.
Fourteen seconds held up by my hair.
My private city. A Barcalounger of DHL cartons.
A mini-piazza for praying. A bingo game.
My hands for sale. Transit maps.
Pigs with umbilicus. Bird without feet.

Keen

if I were to give you something to use
　　　　a pebble
　　　　a hotline

a coupon
little adding machines
suspended in the void
an eye's panorama
taking in the oriental horizon

like the fetal fields in The Matrix
　　　　grown from GMOs
　　　　fueling baby smell

a repairman calls me
a rock star
I'm OK for 8000
"an extra thou" to blow in Mexico
　　　　"and do what"
　　　　and do what
tack on extra a month
mad and abstract
a tanda is a kye
　　　　a new computer
　　　　plus some button-downs
　　　　a half-number, a full
better than a bank
you can corner
the liquor-convenience store
market on the Compton/
Koreatown border
eventually it'll be your number

tanda means old
　　　　"tight"

some summer wheeling
through needy circuits
ingenious in common use
            random burger joints
            Raybans
            "but you won't turn me"

the natural uses of any city
persist in the cracks of
economy
            some say the market is
            some say the market is

To invite the confidence of large contributors

er   errant   when does meaning come   intend

then krump

        barring full audit of your leaky degree

ar   armor   blur at

the edges

ab   abjure

        is there a surgical robot on your building committee

um   bloom

ra   rah rah rah   what is this about

where is it proposed to erect proof of your significance to Letters

re   red   I burn   album

        your replicate sheep collateral

        what can be done with $25,000 in respect to face recognition software

ba   ban

mu   muscle

        if not what assurance have you of continuity of pure action

        as organs strain from year to year

What we mean when we talk ambition

a man, a lank of a man
shank of hair, fistful
cocked to the side
a greeting, a shortfall of hair
woman, hair of magnets
filaments sheening
at my side, you can have him
he's my father, he's a lush.

I'm brilliant, a professor now
now a crooked line.
he's coddled and addled.
I'm making it, straight
(now skipping)
you aren't, for me either.
I decline you, with a hello.
yet want want

hulling out want
wordless, wanting
broken parts snap
something
about counting
poems without words
ordinary, the stream
of ordinary

rib, extract my gift
(lush) my successful friend

associate professor
a small kid, my father
says nothing.
I sing, he says nothing
(a poem without words).
look at
all the photos of you
all laid on end
is three hours, in one room

one, half-hour stretched
to three, in his sights
on repeat, a lifetime.
she, in spotlight
me, on the side
this man some
how, his side under
my hands, arch
of rib, perplex
pound

I wanna be your dog

An old account into the irate
Cross of lettuce sphere
Now more-or-less a career
Milking a head of Cheez Whiz
Hi Ms ________
This is ________
With a T I a crass
Your retirement company
On the fine again
That's morsey poor
With T I A Crap
Lyrics obscene render
Pudenda ruin and urine
We're gonna be face-to-face
I'll lay right down
My favorite place
So messed up I want you
Here in my room I want you
Now I wanna be
Eaten by
Igorots at St. Louis
Now I wanna be
Eaten by
Igorots at St. Louis
Well
C'mon

So I quit

finding new care models to live by
is a new sardonic
relieved to curdle
hoping that low-level humming will
say what social good bodies
aren't invited to say
hoping to escape any brightening up
and trumpets
your white background
your good light
matter "is distributed in bodies"
into an unquiet buzz
by which we know we are
Jello hum churning
and cranked up
howling on YouTube
one screech
knees nose to trumpet bent full
new habits playing
or kinesthetic you jerk

Revive me

Deep infiltration expect constant
        Violate three miles un-heroic
                Happening Cypress Creek Arm
                        Soft stripping

Crossword idling
        Unkind outside musket
                Community offering
                        See my daughters

Helmet French press
        Wet naps west language
                To let chant rhetoric
                        Merrily mess it up hold it

In place just a generation
        Ago they were in the jungle
                Beginning of the sentence
                        Ends in the same medicine

And alphabets afflict a new
        Market the mouth swallow
                Hold in place long note
                        Vanishing point B still

Living little things
        Collected clothes washers
                Danglers buying in
                        Burned

Lovely ends language let
        Into the Good Book
                Annotate split feet from land
                        Rectangular holes punched

Through each blue roof
Fur soften arms guard
Whose how is yours random
Like mine's closed for

Business go see if there's
Interest in reanimating eighteen
Low-income units expected
After several hundred

Razed boring past exterior
Nineteen trees perimeter numbered
114 thru 122 inanimate like
Fingers not circling hips

But some of us are the resound

You so material so networked we

The chronic indebted finish no programs possess no degrees

The half-baked idea author no books win no grants deserve no feedback

The aging on the temporary gig friend no contacts find no mentors schedule no payments

The lazily reverent dispense no advice teach no classes read at no readings

The yelling have no collaborators

The exhausted object have no body of work

The good life

There ought to be a career of slow inhale exhale

There ought to be smoke breaks from self-actualization

Some days we should read nothing

Some days just one sentence

A paid leave from poems working hard

A recess from fundraising

A holiday from our keeping before we were done in

Ask for everything

A phase of eccentric middle-aged dress

Where everywhere and

No event is an occasion

Unfit for a five-piece uniform

Ask everything

Does live-tweeting the death of an industry earn you a job in death

Does pounding out choice conference aphorisms count as community work

Does updating a relentlessly upbeat Facebook feed win you the emerging person's award

Does digital labor create a taste for your pay-walled peer review

Does public vulnerability count as a brand

After after

one long decade
in clutched vestments
overwrites the vapors
lush with ethno-mania
these all process words
relational janitorial
karaoke
glitter a post-
an anti-
a muffin top
re- and de-
thigh touches
dis- the end of -izing
earnest proposals
a half nod
camouflaged precariat
fester and rot
I'm afraid every word
is jargon I can
childish play
like flip you through
relational modes
oh that pessimism
there's grit
emergent sub-
sub-field
karaoke studies
an -ism of a -ness
late to camouflage

she the serious grievance
become subject and simile
a verse to someone or other

All the Pinays are straight, all the queers are Pinoy, but some of us

hold our femme gaze straight into the cosmos

behold a supernova of fat negation

know Mark Aguhar as the real babaylan

have mothers young enough to be our sons never to reach 26

Blessed be

our ugly grief

our helpless beauty

this very moment of utterance incarnate in an absent brown body

joining us

alive painfully so

strand us alone together

I will never not

want to be violent with you (dare you to say

this isn't love, queen)

pray for

her resurrection every easter

"I'm just so bored and so pretty and not white"

LOL YOUR PINAY SELF
LOL YOUR SUBCONSCIOUS DECOLONIAL INDIGENEITY
LOL RECOVERY AS AN ESCAPE HATCH FROM REAL NEGOTIATIONS
LOL CARING THAT WHITE PEOPLE THINK OUR BODIES ARE CHEAP
LOL THINKING ONLY WHITE PEOPLE THINK OUR BODIES ARE CHEAP
LOL THINKING WHITE POETS MATTER AT ALL
LOL FRETTING OVER OUR FAILED TOKENIZATION
LOL AGENCY AND THE COURAGE TO SPEAK
LOL CENTERING OURSELVES IN THE NARRATIVE
LOL PRETTY TRAUMA POETRY AT OUR NATION'S CAPITAL
LOL RESPECTABILITY POLITICS
LOL SLUT SHAMING
LOL LANGUAGE SHAMING
LOL MOTHER TONGUE
LOL THE MOTHERLAND
LOL PRECOLONIAL PARADISE FOLK TALES
LOL UTOPIA UNTOUCHED BY QUEER PINAY RUIN ACROSS TIME & SPACE
LOL YOUR LOLA
LOL YOUR HIYA
LOL YOUR WALANG HIYA
LOL OUR TENDER EMOTIONALITY

Book of ant bites

Every pinched tobacco a two-fingered mudra

Every sign to enter the dead

Some apprenticeships figure eights

Some departments bug eyes

Some search committees infinity

Some symposia HOV lanes

Some lady-scholars Whole Foods

Some cluster cohorts windowless rooms

My slackening beneath star-steam

My entrails a fine sugar trail

My jaw rubbed in mud

My language bitten out of me

My falling unconscious into Spanish

A circle of anthropologists a historian a theater director

A set of twins mother and daughter

A car blaring Bollywood in front of the Cristo Rey

A network of complaints private service announcements & Vines

A table for ladling your enemies some mercy for skinny jeans

A Zyrtec to seal my name

When it snows indifferent to law

From up here we see a lot
          She speaks breathlessly
I built this hermitage with the help
of my brothers   Just a cave
My mind wanders like horses, yaks
and insects
          In the worldly life
          She gathers
firewood   smoke rises from
the cave's chimney
          My plum
coconut ice cream is melting
She comes out smiling
          I've lived here
nine years
without suspendable rights
My prayer flags
on the next full moon
I tie   on my mother
for her four AM devotions
It's very hard to get up here
          in winter
It's also hard when it rains
          I could slide off a cliff
Laying down laws
          other than the law
She climbs the mountain
It doesn't hurt
          Today
          I spent some money
as I did yesterday
As long as I get enough
to eat and can practice
I don't care about anything else
          She is settling in her meditation box

I feel a little repulsed
If the law suspends rights
            for any immeasurable war
any time   we dream
we could ask for predictions
I asked him about myself
            There is a transcript
            Tells of an old
Lady in black leaving
the family house unlocked
retiring   to the servant's hut
in her backyard
            It's not bad at all
The door creaks
we suspend the law
the ocean of sadness
I thought my bones were
breaking
for a year
            a crane pan exploits
the shack's tiny footprint

Court lady sits in a Chevron car wash

On Google trying to remember
Holding a trans rights sign on someone's timeline
Catching an ex in a documentary
Getting face-recognized
In rehearsals subbing for Puck on Instagram
In a zine about revenge
Setting a timer on repeat
Looking at torn-up pages in the woods

On the way to Nueva Filipinas

Over an abyss, approach
with discretion, attention, caution
            in stealth mode,
in dead wells
My transport is
            I think
the tech of the poem
left to earth
found in a Costco
among marked cartons stacked tall
with jarred jellyfish

A regular tomboy-femme cupping a cup
            of joe
an attitude that makes you run
despite fatigue, past fatigue, post-fatigue

Women sitting
on cardboard boxes, pink sheets
hover over Tupperware of food
over the aqueduct, under the overpass
they unpack their shoulders, their shoulders
fan out in long arcs thrown back
scores bubble forth into a laughing river

A City bustles, beeps, smells
opens into infinite
negative space, fries meat, spits out
passengers half-asleep next to
phone card hawkers, moneychangers

The City won't let me alone
tries me out to be its niece,
a light-skinned consumptive
from Santa Scholastica,
a man in dingy crinolines,

solitude being alien
to most Filipinos.

Somewhere in the lower keys
I wink awake
into the silicon valley
of the Comanche
under the cirrus canopy's
thudding shadows
sheltering the dings
of pedicabs

I was born for a stricter regime

than this loose place of acoustic guitar mass and grape juice

trained long before birth to be a soldier of something

a wife of someone's
a link to some underground
a constellation

ready for the call exiled from the cell
embedded missing you
dreaming the word
a passkey magic safe entry

haunting corners scanning my papers for fraud
flushing myself out
terror is the mainstream's peace

I will be truthful I am lost
the mall is starting to make me forget

the prophecy fulfilling itself
a manifesto

in one line indigene in the next struggling with addiction
in each wife and nun

a hand of unraveled threads a bomb blast awhile ago
violence in the soft core

paratroopers I am running out of writing implements

they want to know how I run

Bodies in spaces forced to accommodate

A sea wall fun grows along

A calloused pointing a purple toe

A step back a boot gasp

A brush and a cushion

A dress for shooting

A call to stand loose remnant

A gutter thick and song

A young cloak of

A bamboo shoot and tomb

Virgin origin

a skinny girl
a hole one could stand
in cave-like conditions
Andee slept
14 hours

it's hard to be smart

"a festival" in a
sepia village with lots
of wants
dusty season

it's hard to smarten up

the harshest season
I slept
10 hours
in a hole fit for an upright
coffin
"isn't dead but depressed"

it's hard to smart

A land planted by eyes refusing to be closed

It began with	Seven hens	Fifteen or seven	Manifested monsters
Dark stone	Half-knowledge	No alternatives	Soupy
I provoked	A middle-aged man	Who made me	Feel like a girl
I did whatever	I'd done	Against my better	Judgment
He came at me	Leather skin	White chest fuzz	Pink striped shirt
In the stairwell	To the clamoring	Street below	People like me
Get bruised	In the movies	Playing	Like us
Found	In the northeast	Corner of the city	Possibly a migrant
Throwaway	I heard the cock	Crow in midday	Claiming seven
Neighborhood hens	I thought	Before I did it or	I did it before
I'd thought	My index fingers	In his eyes	Thumbnails in
Nose hairs	Hanging on	For dear life	I did it or I didn't
I still don't know	Starch pressed	Pause before one's	Death
Live on	In montage	Canned soup	Burst from his eyes
My illegal sit	A teakettle	And a school	But no more eyes
To build on desert	He said there is	No other way	Around
What you see	We were born here	Before we arrived	You mustn't say
The name of	This place	It makes me lose	Patience

Call me bee for the king maker

Queened at the deadline
Be very pleased
Figures in my hand
Mean to jumble for mating
Plumb a sick line a sure line to forever
Hate the bathroom's crumbly paste
You the thinly cut suit
The front the side the face
The scrim the half lit
The insurance
These jokes and songs in a circus town
Wontons somehow
You clucked wrist
Downy worry
I verbena Lucite skulking
The gander
The color blue
Cottoning your back pocket
The molting there
Call me bee for the kingmaker
Call for a michelada

I have to tell you

Every segment of an ordinary day is clocked by a chemical reaction
As sentimental minerals attract to our automations.
Any coordinated skill has a soul mate of pure bile.
Every armpit hair a trigger for metal and summer
When the room has a blinded window and scented lotion.
Only the action of walking walks its winding uphill curve
In the shortened shadows the morning after solstice
A man shape swipes me for two dollars.
The train doesn't stop where I'm healing.

Stop at staggered times. Constrict vocal chords
String up crumpled together moments a sea of sound
The stomach a balloon, an accordion, a noisy woodpecker slurred to a drone
A head drifting north to east still oriented.
Follow while going elsewhere.
You answer to a name that's not yours.
After a while, it will become yours.
Face the wall when someone behind you jumps.
Eyelids droop toward eardrums.
I'll cry at the urinals before I cry at your jugular
Only the action of riding is leaving the station.
Staying virgin for a language is a longtime stand-in for my weeping
Even a closed door to cliché is a cliché.

Afterword

This book began on a train between Midwestern libraries. A winter of ash cold metal and bindings with blunted corners. Overheated rooms held archival records of people moving through the real and unreal. I was gathering a kind of global guidebook on everyday life imprinted by U.S. colonial power over the Philippines from 1898 to 1946. My Midwest but before the rust. A completed dissertation led me to Austin, Texas, when the summer sky was a long dry gutter. The air-conditioning unit broke down for two summers. I became impassive. Shadows passed through photocopies arrayed on my floor. I obsessively bid on eBay for mid-luxury handbags and early 1900s children's books. On a one-year fellowship, I lived above a chain smoker in East Urbana, Illinois. Mostly snowed in, I quit smoking for good. I wrote lovesick letters on Tumblr.

This book was written in a collapse of a project. Ordinariness is its own proof of disaster. I commute every workday across two highways and a river and every morning is a time-lapse motion sequence of economic segregation. East to west with the sunrise: third- and fourth-generation Latino and black families empty out their houses and leave East Austin. Seasons pass with razed blocks and condos. Fifteen minutes westward is bright with the super-rich isolating themselves up in the suburban hills. A routine of violence's compression.

We can't stand for proof. We can be fans and haters somewhere alone together, maybe posting comments on each other's comments on something. Under aliases, we recap TV shows, video games, late capitalism, histories of history. A U.S. general's houseboy somewhere on the Pacific Ocean shows up, on his way to be displayed at a Midwestern church fair in the 1920s. What's distracting lately, what's saturating you, what can we hash over together. We egg each other on.

—Kimberly Alidio
Austin, Texas 2016

Kimberly Alidio is a high school teacher and a tenure-track dropout, born in West Baltimore, Maryland and raised in Baltimore County. She is the author of *solitude being alien* (dancing girl press, 2013). She received an artist-in-residency at the Center for Art and Thought, a Zora Neale Hurston Scholarship (Naropa University), an Asian American Studies Postdoctoral Fellowship (University of Illinois), a Pushcart Prize nomination, and poetry fellowships from Kundiman and VONA/Voices. With her partner, kt shorb, she lives in East Austin, Texas.

The cover artist Gina Osterloh (b. 1973) earned her BA from DePaul University in 1996 and her MFA from the University of California, Irvine in 2007. Recent solo exhibitions include *Gina Osterloh* at Higher Pictures, New York (2015), *Nothing To See Here There Never Was* (2015) at Silverlens Gallery in Manila, Philippines, *Press Erase Outline Slice Strike Make An X Prick!* (2014) at François Ghebaly in Los Angeles, *Anonymous Front* (2012) at the Yerba Buena Center for the Arts in San Francisco and *Group Dynamics and Improper Light* (2012) at Los Angeles Contemporary Exhibitions. Osterloh's work was also included in *Fragments of an Unknowable Whole* (2014) at the Urban Arts Space, at Ohio State University and *This Is Not America: Resistance, Protest and Poetics* (2014) at the Arizona State University Art Museum. Recent reviews include *The New Yorker Magazine* and *Artforum*. Osterloh lives in Los Angeles and currently teaches at California State University, Fullerton and Santa Ana College. Her work is represented by Higher Pictures (New York), François Ghebaly (Los Angeles) and Silverlens (Manila, Philippines).

For kt shorb

Acknowledgements

"The ash does not add" was originally published in *La Vague*; sections of "Certainty is a desire" in *Horse Less Press Review*; "Enclosed within a boundary" in *Best of Kore Press*; "Book of ant bites" in *Lingerpost* and appeared in Marisa Johnson-Valenzuela's anthology, *Dismantle*; "The good life," "Ask for everything," "Ask everything," "After after" and "All the Pinays are straight, all the queers are Pinoy, but some of us" in *Matter*; "I was born for a stricter regime" in *Esque*; "Keen" in *Spiral Orb*; and "Revive me" in *Fact-Simile.* "But some of us are the resound" appeared in *#socialmediaanxieties*; "Only mangos and jungle," "In the province," "Servants" and "Solitude being alien" appeared in the Center for Art and Thought's *Sea, Land, Air* exhibit. Several poems were gathered into a chapbook, *solitude being alien*, by dancing girl press.

"All the Pinays are straight, all the queers are Pinoy, but some of us" quotes Mark Aguhar's *Call Out Queen*, and takes its title from Gloria T. Hull, Patricia Bell Scott, and Barbara Smith's *All the Women Are White, All the Blacks Are Men, But Some of Us Are Brave: Black Women's Studies.*

"Bodies in spaces forced to accommodate" takes its title from Ayesha Siddiqi's podcast, *Pushing Hoops with Sticks Vol 2: You're Not Crazy.*

"Certainty is a kind of desire" was written with Stefano Harney and Fred Moten's *The Undercommons*, and was written with found language from the New York Historical Museum, the San Francisco Exploratorium, the Filipino American Historical Society of Chicago, the University of Illinois at Chicago, the Chicago Historical Society, the University of Chicago Theological Seminary Archives, and Paul G. Cressey's "A Comparison of the Roles of the 'Sociological Stranger'" in *Urban Life* 12: no. 1 (1932).

"Cento" was written entirely with found language from Roland Barthes' *A Lover's Discourse*, Judith Butler's *To Sense What is Living in the Other*, Clarice Lispector on the Montevidayo website (October 17, 2012), and Alice Notley's "Epic & Women Poets" and *Descent of Alette.*

"Daddy Burger Snow Copernicus" contains a loosely translated line from Aldir Blanco & João Bosco's "O Almirante Negro."

"Do you want vitamins?" was written with language found in Dada Docot's documentary video, *Balikbayan*.

"Enclosed within a boundary" was written almost entirely with language found in the holdings of the U.S. Navy and Civil Government records on Guam and on instruction signs at the National Archives-Pacific Region, San Bruno, California.

"I wanna be your dog" was written with The Stooges' song of the same name and refers to the 1904 St. Louis Worlds Fair exhibits of Filipino Cordillerans performing dog-eating rituals.

"In the province" was written with found language from the Bentley Historical Library and Victor Heiser's *An American Doctor's Odyssey.*

"A land planted by eyes refusing to be closed" takes its title from Etel Adnan's "Jebu" in *To look at the sea is to become what one is*, edited by Thom Donovan and Brandon Shimoda.

"Now I will behold a whole tropical story" was written with found language from John Stuart Thomson's *Fil and Filippa.*

"On the way to Nueva Filipinas" was written after Marisa González's video, *Female open space invaders 1* and with found language from Luis Francia's "In Search of the Tadtarin" in the *Philippine Inquirer* (August, 18, 2010).

"Primly inside a melon zone" was written with found language from Emory S. Bogardus' "Filipino Immigrant Attitudes" in *Sociology and Social Research XIV* (May-June 1930), Ella Barrows Hagar's *Continuing Memoirs*, and Bruno Lasker's *Filipino Immigration to the United States and Continental Hawaii.*

"Servants" was written entirely with found language from newspapers on *Chronicling America.*

"So I quit" contains a line from Francis Bacon's *The History of Dense and Rare.*

"To invite the confidence of large contributors" was written with found language from the National Archives, College Park, Maryland.

"To turn insurgents into state agents" was written entirely with found language from *PRI America Abroad*'s interviews with General Stanley McChrystal, historian Max Boot, journalist Rajiv Chandrasekaran, and Colonel Peter Mansoor.

"When it snows indifferent to law" was written with found language from Bari Pearlman's documentary, *Daughters of Wisdom.*

Thank you to Marthe Reed and everyone at Black Radish Press. Thank you to my poet-guide, Hoa Nguyen. Thank you to my long-time fellow writer, Sarita See. Thanks to the Alidio families, Beverly Bajema, Ruth Nicole Brown, Clare Counihan, Robert Devens, Dot Devota, the late Bhante Suhita Dharma, Lara Durback, May Fu, Samantha Giles, Sarah Heady, Christine Shan Shan Hou, Mushim Ikeda, Liz Kinnamon, Joseph Legaspi, Muriel Leung, David Lloyd, Fred Moten, Mónica Teresa Ortiz, Jason Magabo Perez, Lilia Rosas, Mardee Rosuello, Jon Salunga, Andee Scott, Brandon Shimoda, the Shorb families, Emji Spero, Eileen Tabios, Wendy Vastine, and Yael Villafranca